MEASURING

FIRST MATHS

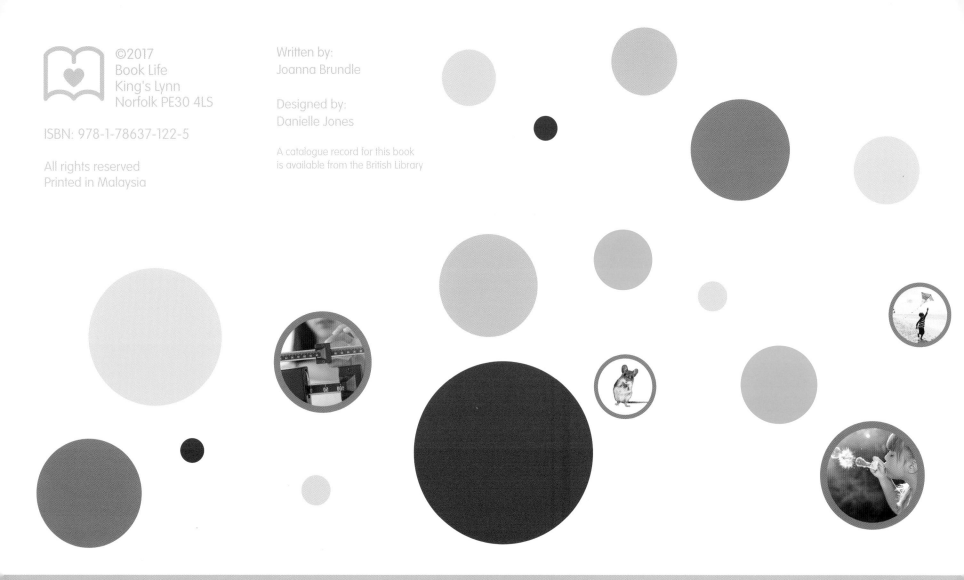

©2017
Book Life
King's Lynn
Norfolk PE30 4LS

ISBN: 978-1-78637-122-5

Written by:
Joanna Brundle

Designed by:
Danielle Jones

A catalogue record for this book
is available from the British Library

PHOTO CREDITS

CONTENTS

LENGTH

Long Hair

Short Hair

Length is how long something is.

This girl is measuring the length of her arm with a tape measure.

HEIGHT

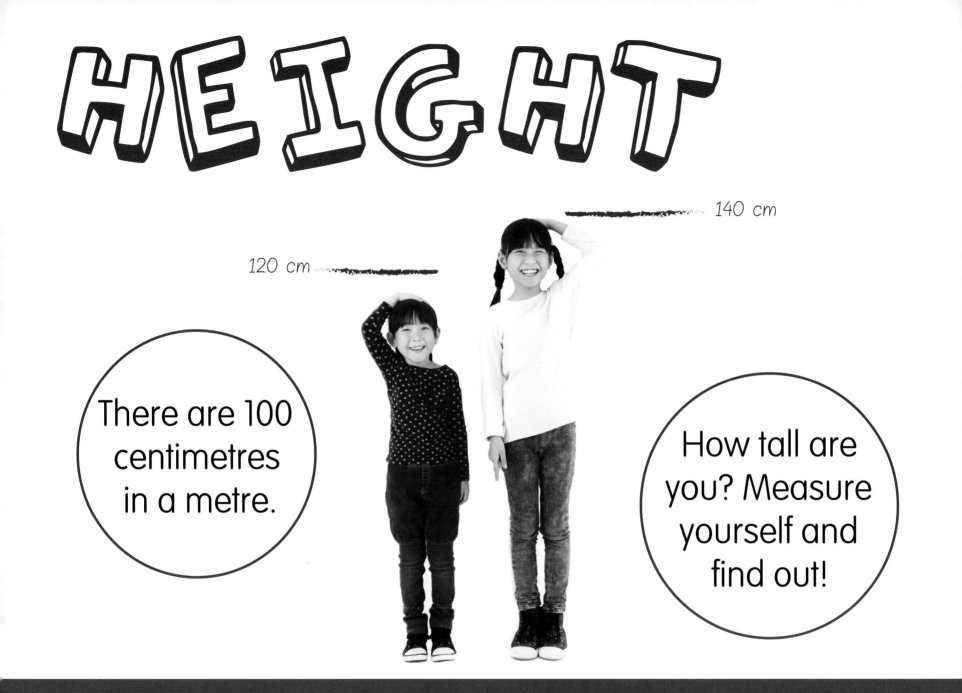

140 cm

120 cm

There are 100 centimetres in a metre.

How tall are you? Measure yourself and find out!

Height is how tall something is.

A giraffe can be the same height as a tree.

WIDTH

This man is using a tape measure to measure the width of a door.

Width is how wide something is.

The bridge is the same width as the river.

DISTANCE

This woman is about to run a 100 metre race.

Distance is how far apart two things are.

It's 13 kilometres from the sign to Dublin.

SPEED

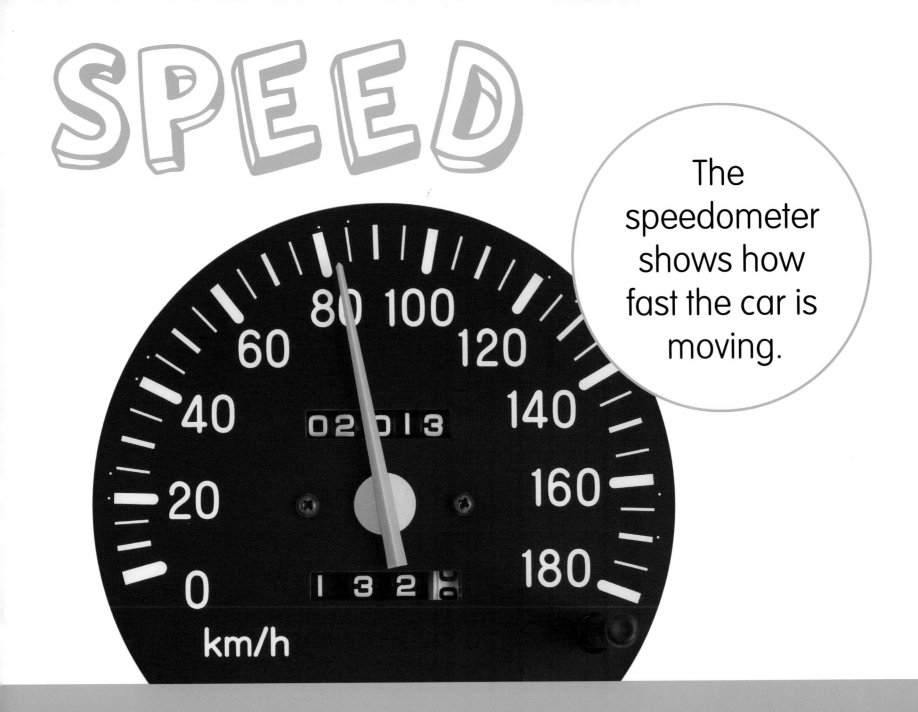

The speedometer shows how fast the car is moving.

Speed is how quickly something moves.

A cheetah can run at nearly 100 kilometres per hour. That's fast!

TIME

Hour Hand

Minute Hand

Second Hand

Time is how long something takes.
Clocks and watches help us to measure time.

Destination	Time
LONDON	10:25
PARIS	11:05
MADRID	11:40
NEW YORK	
AMSTERDAM	
VENICE	

What time does the aeroplane for London leave?

Measuring time tells us when things will happen.

WEIGHT

Scales

Weight is how heavy something is.
We use scales to measure weight.

We use scales to weigh ingredients when we are baking.

TEMPERATURE

Nurse's Thermometer

96.7

We use a thermometer to measure temperature.
The temperature of something is how hot or cold it is.

A thermometer in ice measures the temperature as below zero degrees Celsius. That's cold!

UNUSUAL MEASUREMENTS

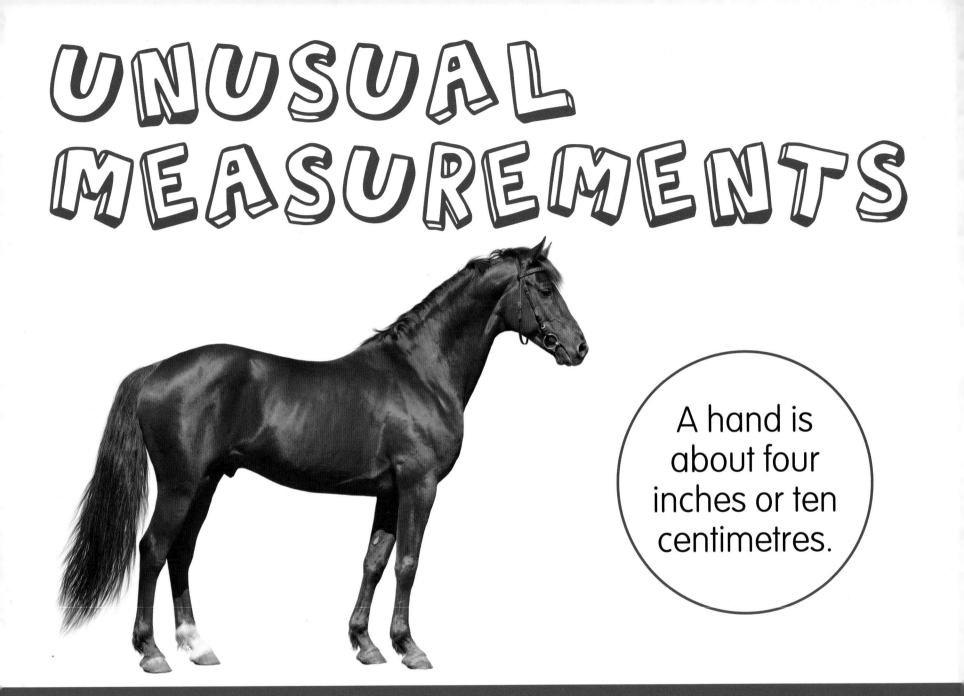

A hand is about four inches or ten centimetres.

The height of a horse is measured in hands.

A knot is just slower than two kilometres per hour.

At sea, speed is measured in knots.

MEASURING AND COMPARING

Point to the tallest dog.

Point to the shortest dog.

Which one do you think weighs the most?

Which is the fastest, a bicycle, a car or an aeroplane?

FUN THINGS TO DO

Working with a friend, measure your lunch boxes. Weigh the things inside. How heavy is an apple in grams?

Use a stopwatch to see how long it takes your friend to run to the end of the playground. Then swap over. Who is faster?